101

ways

to
rock

**SOLO FEMALE
TRAVEL**

101 ways to rock

SOLO FEMALE TRAVEL

Move past your fears,
empower yourself, and have fun!

charyn pfeuffer with
dayna steele & jenny block

Daily Success
THE BOOK SERIES

101 WAYS TO ROCK SOLO FEMALE TRAVEL
Copyright 2019 Daily Success LLC

Back cover author photo credit:
Charyn Pfeuffer - Alex Garland
Dayna Steele – Dack Justiz
Jenny Block – Steph Grant

ISBN print 978-1-7337924-6-2
ISBN ePUB 978-1-7337924-7-9
ISBN MOBI 978-1-7337924-8-6

The tips in this book are merely suggestions. Because of the
dynamic nature of the Internet, any Web addresses or links
contained in this book may have changed since publication
and may no longer be valid. The views expressed in this work
are solely those of the author and do not necessarily reflect
the views of the publisher, and the publisher hereby disclaims
any responsibility for them. Travel at your own risk.

PRINTED IN THE UNITED STATES OF AMERICA
PUBLISH DATE NOVEMBER 2019

Publisher contact and book orders:
Daily Success Publishing
1400 McKinney Street
Suite 2110
Houston TX 77010
info@101waystorock.com
www.101waystorock.com

For my mother, Christine Ayn Pfeuffer, whose end-of-life regret, "I never went to Europe," sparked a lifetime of wanderlust.
- Charyn Pfeuffer

101 WAYS TO ROCK BOOK SERIES
101 Ways to Rock Online Dating
Havana: 101 Ways to Rock Your World
LinkedIn: 101 Ways to Rock Your World
In the Classroom: 101 Ways to Rock Your World
Welcome to College! 101 Ways to Rock Your World
On the Golf Course: 101 Ways to Rock Your World
and the original
101 Ways to Rock Your World:
Everyday Activities for Success Everyday

Travel is the movement of people between distant geographical locations. Travel can be done by foot, bicycle, automobile, train, boat, bus, airplane, ship or other means, with or without luggage, and can be one way or round trip.
-Wikipedia definition

PACK YOUR BAGS

By Charyn Pfeuffer

In 1990, my mother, Christine Ayn Pfeuffer sighed in a Percocet daze, "I never went to Europe. And I can never have sex again." It was a Thursday night, two weeks before her 38-year old body conceded its brief battle with lung cancer.

Despite losing my go-to guide for all things female, I've powered off my mother's end-of-life regret these past 20-some years: *find your Europe and go there now.*

A few years after my mother's death, I cashed my sophomore year student loan check and bought two round-trip tickets to London and Eurail Passes. I convinced my girlfriend Juliette to take the semester off. We hatched plans to travel through England, France, Spain, Italy, Germany, Switzerland, Belgium and Amsterdam. I rationalized that the trip would honor my mother's end of life regret. My father deemed the adventure reckless.

Juliette's and my trip to Europe set the stage for a life of wanderlust, curiosity and looking to other cultures to learn. Abroad, the more people I interacted with, the more understanding I accrued. I believe these interactions made (and still make) me a kinder, more empathetic person and a better citizen of the earth. In the time it would've taken to complete a semester, it became clear to me that the world is the greatest classroom – not a college environment. I believed I would learn more by traveling than I ever could from a textbook or lecture. Life is an adventure. The minute you kill curiosity, you're screwed. That trip made me hungry for more and turning that crazy idea into a career has been one of my best decisions.

In 2013, Lisa Ling gave a speech at Tufts University, after which students asked her what advice she had for young people.

"The best education I have ever received was through travel," said the California-based journalist. "You'll become more conversant, poised and smarter."

Until a few years ago, I was by most travelers' standards a bona fide jetsetter, logging 100-plus flights per year. I jaunted far and wide, stayed at the swankiest hotels, saw the world's best sights, and attended once-in-a-lifetime events.

Think traveling Spain with one of the country's most sought after winemakers, Maria Martinez-Sierra of Bodegas Montecillo. Exploring the cerulean blue waters of Bonaire with scuba pioneer Dr. Sylvia Earle. Kicking back cocktails until all hours with celebrity chefs like Bobby Flay, Ming Tsai, Tom Collicchio at the *Food & Wine Classic* in Aspen. Cooking traditional Andean recipes with my sweet Peruvian friend Ernesto's mother and sister in Cusco. Taking the Terrible Towel to Machu Picchu, then crossing paths with offensive lineman Chris Keamoeatu at the Royal Hawaiian on Oahu a few weeks after the Steelers won the 2008 Super Bowl. (I gave him a copy of the photo.) And that's just a small glimpse of the greatness I got to experience.

Despite the success of *memoirs Wild* and *Eat, Pray, Love*, the concept of women traveling alone isn't new. Booking.com found that 65% of American women are booking solo travel trips. Throughout the ages, women have pursued wanderlust — following their dreams, falling in love, and learning more about the world. Still, females are subjected to scrutiny that men aren't when flying solo. Incredulous comments like, "He lets you travel by yourself?" and "Aren't you afraid?" often surround such unaccompanied adventures.

Travel awakens my whole being and makes me take notice of my surroundings. It tears me from my comfort zone and often presents unimaginable challenges. I tend to crave all things extreme and exciting and think I'm at my best when I'm forced to spin stress into success. It can be disconcerting, maddening and even scary at times, but every time I do something I didn't think possible, I am thankful for an opportunity to push my personal limits.

Yes, there can be some uncomfortable moments in traveling alone, such as unwanted attention or stretches of solitude. The upsides and empowerment far outweigh the "what ifs" that threaten to keep you home. This book will give solo female travelers the tools to travel capably and confidently – all by yourself.

Now, go on and get out there! There's a big wide world out there waiting to be explored. And when you do go, be sure to send us a postcard. Our address is at the end of this book!

101 ways to rock

SOLO FEMALE TRAVEL

If you don't get out of the box you've been raised in, you won't understand how much bigger the world is.

- Angelina Jolie

1

Travel on your own terms

By default, group travel necessitates compromise. If you have ever traveled with friends or family, you know firsthand the frustration of having to navigate the demands of other people's wants, needs, and schedules. The beauty of solo travel is that you have the freedom to do anything, anytime, and put your needs first. Fall in love with a city and want to spend a few extra days? You can do it – without disrupting the schedule of others.

2

Figure out where and how you want to travel

If you have your heart set on a particular destination, it is crucial to figure out the "where" of your trip first. The next detail to nail down is your travel style. Are you a low-key traveler, or do you prefer luxury experiences? Take this into consideration when you start to think about how much the trip will actually cost.

3

If you can be flexible on the destination...

Since you do not need to coordinate plans with others, you have the luxury of snagging last-minute deals. Use search tools like Kayak or Skyscanner, which allow you to search flights to "anywhere." If you are on a budget and OK with spontaneity, this is one way to save money.

A cruise is one of the best gifts you can give yourself as a solo traveler. Think of it: Time to yourself on the ship, where you can hit the spa or simply lounge by the pool, drink in hand. In ports, you can take an excursion with other people – or simply explore on your own. You can eat what you want when you want. And the best thing is that it's easy to meet people if you wish – at trivia sessions, wine tastings or other onboard activities. What are you waiting for?

- Chris Gray Faust, managing editor, Cruise Critic

4

Cruising is an excellent option for solo travelers

In this coupled-up world, cruising is an excellent option if you like the idea of solo travel, but do not want to deal with logistics. The safety element of your trip is built in: You know where you are going to sleep every night, and there is a network of support on board should you need a doctor or concierge.

5

Practice makes perfect

If you have never traveled on your own, it is a good idea to take a dry run before you plan a more ambitious adventure. The best place to practice is near where you live. For example, if you live in Seattle, WA, try a solo weekend away in Vancouver, BC or Portland, OR. That way, you will get comfortable with dining and exploring in your own company before taking on any big solo adventures.

To travel is worth any cost or sacrifice.

- Elizabeth Gilbert, author of *Eat Pray Love*

6

Budget for your trip

If the fact that you are traveling is more important than where and how then start by figuring
out how much money you are willing to spend.
Travel does not have to be prohibitively expensive, and the internet has made it easy to scout
out killer deals on flights, dining, and accommodations. To budget for your trip, start with
the big-ticket expenses (think transportation
and accommodations) and work down to the
smaller ones (like maps and museum tickets).
Since you are probably going to make a lot
of changes in the planning process, use a
spreadsheet to calculate your budget so you
can adjust as you go.

If planning to go on safari, avoid summers and holidays. To secure a spot in the top lodges, it's in November, after the migration in Tanzania and Kenya. Botswana and South Africa's sweet spot is in early December.

- Karen Loftus, international comedian, travel writer and Adventuress in Chief at Women's Adventure Travels (www.womensadventuretravels.com) Instagram @womensadventuretravels

7

Consider traveling during shoulder or off-season

If you are flexible on timing, shift your dates to the shoulder or off-season. Think ski trips during mud season, or that sweet spot right after peak powder season. Or destinations south of the equator during their winter season, where weather may be slightly cooler, thus, tickets will be cheaper. Typically, January is the cheapest month to travel.

I'm someone who travels for food experiences. Before I leave for a trip, I make sure to get tips from restaurant industry pals, fellow writers, social media friends, and I love doing a call-out to my tablehopper subscribers for recommendations!

- Marcia Gagliardi, founder,
tablehopper.com

8

Are you a foodie?

This is an expense that will vary from person to person, depending upon priorities. If going to the restaurants of Michelin-starred chefs is your thing, build luxe culinary experiences into your budget. If you are happy cooking for yourself or picnicking with a baguette and a bottle of wine, your food budget will be far less. This is one area of solo travel where you can save or splurge.

9

Buy tickets and book experiences in advance

Whether it is going whale watching or attending a Broadway play, it is rare to go somewhere and not rack up expenses for activities and entertainment. It is essential to budget for these experiences. It may be less expensive to purchase tickets for these events before you go. Popular deal sites like Groupon and LivingSocial offer deep discounts. For theatergoers who want to attend shows spur of the moment, "rush" is the general term for day-of, first-come-first-serve seats sold at the theater box office.

Generosity is the best investment.
- Diane Von Furstenberg

10

Factor gratuities into your budget

When you travel in the US, tipping is expected when you dine out or visit a spa. Tipping customs vary widely in other countries, so it is important to research local customs before you go. Be sure to bring small bills so you can tip. My advice is, if someone touches it, you tip them. This means everyone from the bellman to the bartender. As far as we are concerned, every experience that involves a hard-working human deserves a tip – even if it is just a few bucks.

11

Walking-around money

Many incidental expenses can occur throughout your trip, from snacks to sunblock. Set aside
a small daily contingency fund for all the little
extras that pop up along the way.

12

Build an extra financial cushion for safety

It is important to budget extra money for safety precautions. If your flight lands late at night, it is worth the added expense of booking a hotel that will pick you up at the airport or paying a little extra to stay in a place that is centrally located (and well-reviewed). If things really go sideways, you should have enough money (or credit) to buy yourself an overpriced, last-minute ticket home.

Morocco is a notoriously difficult destination for solo female travel, so I wanted to do as much research as possible before my trip. It took less than an hour for that legwork to come in handy: After my transfer never showed for my 11:30 pm airport pick-up in Casablanca – and a call to the hotel provided zero help – it was time for my back-up plan. Instead of panicking, I headed outside to the taxi stand, knowing that I needed to agree on the fare with the driver before getting in his car. (And I knew what that price should be, so I wasn't overcharged.) Another pro tip: Don't let anyone offer to carry your luggage to the taxi stand – they'll expect a hefty tip in return. Simple research can save you from anxious scrambling at the last minute.

- Amy Cassell,
travel writer, and editor

13

Learn about your destination

Like going into most situations in life, it is best to be prepared. Take the time to research the status of your destination with the State Department. Also read up on rules of etiquette, common local crimes, safe and unsafe areas, and the local political landscape. It is also smart to program local emergency numbers into your phone.

14

Study a map before you go

Spend some time looking at local routes to get a handle on your destination. Use Google Maps to locate not only fun landmarks and restaurants, but also the local hospital, police station, and US Embassy. Wi-Fi is not always available, so having even the most basic of bearings can come in handy. Also, having a vague idea of where you are staying, and the location of the nearest public transportation stops can be helpful.

15

Download offline maps

Wi-Fi isn't always a given and carrying a giant paper map signals predators that you are a tourist. Download maps to your phone or iPod, so you do not have to rely on Wi-Fi or a local sim card to get around.

I always purchase travel insurance to cover non-refundable costs such as cruises and prepaid tours. It provides trip cancellation insurance in case I need to cancel for an unexpected medical reason, but also medical insurance while traveling, which is essential since your medical insurance at home may not cover you abroad or even in another state. You also get an emergency number to call, which is nice for peace of mind when you're traveling solo.

**- Sheri Doyle, Pacific Northwest Journeys,
Virtuoso Travel Advisor**

16

Ponder insurance before you wander

When you travel, anything can and will happen, and it is always a good idea to have a safety net in place. Protect your investment – and yourself – with travel insurance. Policies tend to cover specific perils (like a hurricane or medical evacuation) or "cancel for any reason" scenarios. Your credit card, car insurance, or medical insurance may also cover part of your trip. Two excellent online sites to compare benefits are Squaremouth.com and TravelInsurance.com.

17

Check your passport expiration date

Having a soon-to-be expired passport is one of the worst scenarios that can play out at an airport. The U.S. Department of State recommends that your passport is valid for at least six months beyond your actual travel date to avoid lengthy, and potentially expensive, travel disruptions. Our advice? Play it safe and pretend your passport expires six months before it actually expires. If you are departing or returning within six months of the expiration date, you will not be allowed to board a plane in the U.S. Also, check passport requirements in advance with a reliable source, like the U.S Department of State's country site, to make sure all travel documents are valid.

18

Check visas and entry requirements

Before you travel, check visas and entry requirements, and make sure you build in a wider margin than the actual scope of your trip. If you are planning on visiting multiple countries, be sure to scout out the entry requirements and apply for any necessary visas before you leave to avoid any last-minute stress at the customs desk.

19

If you are a U.S. citizen traveling abroad, enroll your trip with the Smart Traveler Enrollment Program (STEP)

This is a super simple and oft-overlooked safety precaution. If you are traveling abroad, register with the STEP program (https://step.state. gov/step). Created by the U.S. Department of State, it literally takes two minutes to fill out the online form and download the app (free; iOS & Android). If something newsworthy goes down (think current travel warnings and alerts) in your foreign destination, they will be the first to let you or a contact at home know. It also gives contact information for U.S. embassies and consulates.

20

If traveling abroad, ask your doctor if any vaccinations are recommended or required.

Before you travel abroad, be sure to check your vaccination status. Use the Centers for Disease Control and Prevention destination tool (wwwnc. cdc.gov/travel/destinations/list) to figure out which vaccines and medications are required or recommended for your trip. Schedule an appointment with a travel medicine specialist at least one month in advance, so you have ample time to fully protect against disease.

21

Check currency conversions

You know the drill. You arrive in a foreign country after a long flight ready to grab your bags, head to the hotel, and take a nap. But you need some cash in local currency to hail a cab and for the various inevitable tips that stand between touch down and check-in. Your knee-jerk reaction is to head straight to the nearest currency exchange kiosk to make the swap, but you may not get the best exchange rate. Take two seconds to find out what the competitive currency exchange rate is before your trip (www.xe.com/ucc). A lot of times, it makes the most sense to hit the closest ATM to grab whatever cash you need (check with your bank for international rates) until you get where you are going.

22

Let your bank and credit cards know you are traveling

Before you travel to any foreign country, alert your bank and set up a travel notice on your credit cards. To prevent fraud, your credit card issuer keeps tabs on your spending activity. If it notices new locations or suspicious spending activity, like a big-ticket purchase (hello, hotel charges!), it may decline a transaction or freeze your card. It is still possible to have your purchases declined after setting a travel notice, but it is far less likely.

23

Get a good travel credit card

Travel rewards credit cards allow users to earn miles and points with regular purchases but do not underestimate the value of the card's benefits program. Some people only focus on the sign-up bonus or points and miles rewards when picking a credit card, but they might be missing out on some critical features. In addition to points and miles, credit cards can offer a slew of benefits that can save you money, including rental car insurance, trip cancellation or interruption insurance, and reimbursement for lost or late luggage. Other awesome perks can include airport lounge access and paid Global Entry/TSA PreCheck membership fees. The best source for comparing travel credit cards is The Points Guy (https://thepointsguy.com); search "Credit Card Guide."

24

Check your mobile phone plan

Roaming charges are one big money-sucking black hole. Of course, you need your mobile phone to survive while on the road; however, be smart about it. If you are traveling domestically, check how much data you have on your current plan, and adjust as needed if you won't have Wi-Fi access or think you will want more. It is much easier to increase your data plan for a month than getting hit with hefty overage fees. Tip: If you are traveling internationally, turn off data roaming before you go, or you will end up with a huge bill. Some mobile phone providers offer reasonable daily global data fees; be sure to check with yours before you go, so you do not have any surprises.

25

Check your health coverage

In the event, you need medical care while traveling (fingers crossed you do not), make sure you know what your health insurance will and won't cover. If you have a pre-existing medical condition, you may want to plan ahead and familiarize yourself with in-network doctors and hospitals at your destination. If you are traveling abroad, your insurance may not offer coverage. If that is the case, many private companies provide short-term, emergency coverage plans, geared toward international travel.

26

Take photos of your most important documents

Snap pics of your key documents, like your passport, credit cards, prescriptions, driver's license, and itinerary and be sure to send them to yourself and upload to the cloud. For backup, leave a copy with a friend or family member back home, just in case you need a copy sent to you.

When traveling, many people working in the tourist-filled areas tend to speak some English, however, don't assume this is always the case. Don't be the "Ugly American" and always ask politely first. Probably the most helpful tool when traveling to a foreign country where you don't speak the language is to be nice. When you're nice, people instinctively want to help even when there is a language barrier present.

- Raquel Segura, president, and
CEO of Je Suis. PARIS Tours

27

Learn the fundamentals of the local language

If you are traveling to a different country, take time to learn common local expressions and courtesies. Not only does it serve a practical purpose, but it can also help earn respect from locals (even if your delivery isn't perfect). Luckily, we exist in a time where there is an abundance of language apps. Duolingo is a widely popular go-to.

28

Pack light

To lighten your load, wear layers, pack convertible clothes, and leave the heavy items at home. There is no place for one-hit-wonder outfits if you are looking to be less burdened. If you are flying, wear your bulkiest shoes on the plane. The most important thing is to be able to carry your luggage all by yourself.

Weather can be so fickle — even if you're a self-proclaimed meteorologist, you never know just what it's going to do! If you're going to rock it as a solo traveler, you'd best be prepared for everything and pack layers just in case.

- Heather MacIntyre

29

Pack for a variety of weather situations

If you plan to travel to a place with varying temperatures, plan accordingly. It's essential to think about what fabrics you're packing. For warm locales, light and airy materials will dry fast and keep you cool. If you're headed to colder climates, thermals are your friend. Think leggings to long-sleeve tees that can be layered. Wherever you go, always pack an outer layer that will protect from wind and rain.

30

Invest in a decent pair of walking shoes

The best shoes for travel are comfortable shoes. Even the smallest blister can slow you down. Put your best foot forward by buying a comfy pair of walking shoes (and breaking them in beforehand). ASICS, Merrell, and New Balance all offer styles that are both cute and comfortable. Dance in them, do the laundry in them, but please, do not ever pack a pair of brand-new shoes for a trip. We pinky swear promise you will regret it.

31

Find a convertible dress that works from day to night

Dresses are a travel no-brainer. They are versatile, easy to pack, and can be worn from the boardwalk to the ballet, with a few accessories. Think sneakers by day; swap out for cute sandals at night. The best travel dresses are made from wrinkle-resistant fabrics, like knit, wool, Spandex, or polyester.

32

Leave the expensive items at home

Do you really need to bring the Fendi handbag? The flashy jewelry? The expensive sunglasses? Sure, these items might look fabulous, but they scream out, "Steal me!" The simplest rule is: Do not pack anything you're not willing to lose. There are plenty of functional bags, faux jewelry, and affordable sunglass brands on the market – advertising wealth and status is not worth the risk.

33

Buy a power bank

A power bank can be a lifesaver when you are on the road or in the friendly skies. At some point, your devices will likely need a charge. You may not be near a power source or want to get stuck to a wall socket when you could be out exploring instead. A portable charger can juice up your phone or camera battery and keep you connected when you need it most.

34

Pick up a few extra small travel locks

You never know when a few small travel locks may come in handy. Bring one for each piece of luggage, and an extra for hostel or train station lockers. Combination locks are preferable to keyed locks, since carrying keys is one more thing to think about (and potentially lose) when traveling.

35

Pack prescription drugs in your carry-on

Go ahead and pack any prescription drugs in your carry-on bag (in their clearly labeled, original containers, of course). You never know when a checked bag may go missing. Transportation Security Administration (TSA) allows travelers to transport unlimited amounts of pills and reasonable quantities of liquid meds in either your carry-on or checked bags. (Ninety days' worth of medication is considered the standard for a "personal supply.") Medicine in a liquid form more than 3.4 ounces (again, in reasonable quantities) does not need to be put in a quart-sized bag.

36

Make sure over the counter (OTC) medicines are legal

A lot of Americans don't realize that some OTC medicines commonly used in the United States could be considered unlicensed or controlled substances in other countries. (Each country has its own guidelines about which medicines are legal.) Some of these drugs include inhalers and some allergy and sinus medications. Specifically, products that contain stimulants (medicines that contain pseudoephedrine such as Actifed, Sudafed, and Vicks inhalers), or codeine are generally prohibited. Before you go, it is best to check with the foreign embassy of the country you will be visiting or passing through to make sure your medicines are permitted in that country.

37

Bring a small first aid kit

Whether you are going camping or to Cabo San Lucas, it is worth the weight to pack a few remedies for common ailments. Bring Band-Aids, an antibiotic ointment, Hydrocortisone for bug bites and rashes, a pain reliever, such as Advil or Tylenol, an antihistamine for allergic reactions, and if rough water or bumpy roads make you queasy, Dramamine. Also, if you are sexually active, straight or bisexual, and traveling abroad, bring emergency contraception, which isn't easy to find internationally.

38

Always give yourself extra time

This is not the most exciting of tips, but it is an important one and totally free. Always plan for more time than what you think is necessary. Whether it is getting to the airport or to a dinner reservation, a plethora of other unforeseen snafus can throw you off your perfectly timed schedule. With a cushion of time on your side, you will be less rushed and better able to enjoy your travels.

39

Think about logistics

If you are anything like us, you feel better when you know precisely what you are walking into. As much fun as it is to plan a greatest hits reel of museums and restaurants to visit, there are some critical logistics to consider before a trip. How am I going to get from the airport to my hotel? Do I need foreign currency? How late can I check-in? Trust us, we are all for improvisation, but going on vacation without thinking about the basics can lead to unnecessary stress.

40

Download Rome2rio

This smart transportation app (rome2rio.com) compares different modes of transport in any city, town, landmark, attraction, or address across the globe – all in one search. Whether you are taking a bike, bus, plane, or train, Rome2rio will get you from point A to point B on the best route possible.

I find taking the time to focus on long, deep inhales and slow exhales – especially in long security line ups – keeps me calm, patient, and connected to my body. Making for a much more grounded travel experience.

- Angela Thurston,
Erotic Mastery Coach

41

Keep your cool

Let's face it; traveling can bring about a sense of panic. Things can, and do, go awry. If you can approach these situations with a calm, cool, and collected attitude, you will be better equipped to deal with everything from lost luggage to canceled flights. If you find yourself feeling overwhelmed, take five deep breaths in and out, and imagine the stress leaving your body with every exhale.

42

Keep your passport on your person

Do not keep your passport in your luggage; keep it on your person, either in a bra wallet or hidden day pack. If your bag gets stolen, you still want to have documentation – literally on your person. Always bring a photocopy of your passport, as well as a back-up form of identification and some emergency cash. You can never be too cautious.

43

Try to arrive and depart during daylight hours

Whenever possible, avoid landing in a new place after dark. If you are a visual person and like to get the lay of the land as soon as possible, arriving after dark can be disconcerting. If you must arrive at night, it is always best to arrange transport with your hotel or an Uber to ensure safe arrival. (We are all for using ride shares and public transportation – once you have gotten a handle on your environs.) Also, be sure to have all your hotel information, as well as a phone number for the driver written down in case your phone dies or stops working.

The last thing you want to do, especially after a long journey, is try to figure out where to stash your stuff and catch a shower. Even if you would like to keep your accommodation plans more flexible, making sure you have a place reserved to relax and regroup as you start your trip is always of benefit.

- Kayt Sukel,
author of *The Art of Risk*, and former partner at award-winning family travel website, Travel Savvy Mom.

44

Always have a solid first-night plan

It is a wise idea always to have the first night of a trip sorted out. It can be risky to arrive in a new place, especially after hours, without a place to stay. At the very least, make a hotel reservation for the first night in every new destination, so you have the peace of mind of a bed and a shower.

45

Buy a SIM card at the airport

Depending on where you are traveling, buying a Subscriber Identity Module, or SIM card (a small plastic card that goes inside any phone that uses the Global System of Mobile Communications, or GSM) at the airport is often a cheap and easy option to stay connected. Make sure that your phone is unlocked before you go so that you can install SIM cards along the way.

46

Keep your bearings

Be prepared to be bombarded the minute you step off the bus, train, or out of the airport. Seriously, these can hands-down be some of the most overwhelming moments of solo travel. It is always good to have an idea of where you are and where you need to go next (whether it's to hail a taxi or which direction to walk). If you need a few minutes to get your bearings, walk a short distance away and take a few deep breaths before making any quick decisions.

47

Carry emergency cash

It is always a good idea to carry a stash of emergency cash in the local currency. (If you pack your own currency, you may have to pay a hefty premium, since the recipient has to exchange it.) We have been stuck in countless destinations where banks have been closed, or ATMs have been inoperable. It is a terrible feeling to be without cash, especially since not every circumstance is credit card friendly.

48

Carry a whistle in your bag

If you are in danger, a whistle is a universally recognized alert signal. Pepper spray is also an excellent self-defense precaution, and legal in all 50 states, but regulated abroad. Bugspray is also an effective (and legal) replacement.

49

Always opt for public transport in a foreign city

Be warned: tourists are a taxi driver's cash cow. Once you have touched down in a new destination, it is tempting to jump into the first taxicab you find. Taxi drivers have been known to exploit tourists for their presumed lack of knowledge and charge exorbitant rates. If it is available, always opt for public transport. Today, most cities, especially within Europe, boast efficient and affordable metro lines. It should go without saying – never accept a ride from a stranger.

50

Keep your luggage with you

If you decide to take a taxi, put your stuff in the
back seat, instead of the trunk, so you have
agency over when you can get out. If you need
to make a quick exit, for whatever reason, you
can grab your things and go.

51

Unless you are renting a vehicle...

Before you spend a bunch of money on rental car insurance, you will want to see whether you are already covered by your own car insurance and/or credit card benefits. Your current auto insurance policy will likely cover the personal use of a rental car, but probably not in most places outside the U.S.

52

Use apps

Your smartphone can be your best (safety) friend. Free apps like Chirpey, RedZone, TripWhistle, and Spotted by Locals, provide everything from digital communities that connect women with similar travel plans and city guides curated by locals to forums with reports of unsafe situations in an area.

53

Hotels vs. Airbnbs?

Opting for a nontraditional means of accommodation is financially appealing and may also offer an experience you may not get staying in a hotel. Over 80% of millennials claim they favor Airbnb over hotels for its ability to provide unique travel experiences that offer a more 'local' experience. Lodging is a big part of any travel budget, and Airbnbs offer value, especially when it includes a kitchen, Wi-Fi, and laundry services. If you're nervous about booking an Airbnb, consider using an Airbnb Superhost. Superhosts must host at least 10 trips a year, maintain at least a 90 percent response rate, receive five-star reviews 80 percent of the time, and not cancel their reservations

54

If you are on a tight budget, consider couch surfing

For those looking for local immersion, Couch-surfing.com is a niche alternative for accommodations, geared mostly toward a younger subset of travelers. The basic gist? Hosts offer a couch or shared living space, completely free of charge. Locals who host out their home to guests are looking to have a cultural exchange by getting to know travelers from all over the world. You can also use the site to find weekly events in many cities. To protect yourself and ensure that you have the best experience, only book with hosts that have been well-reviewed by a good number of travelers.

55

Write it down

Grab a business card or write down the exact address of where you're staying and stash it in a safe place in case your phone dies or gets lost or stolen.

56

Use mobile check-in
if available

If mobile registration is available at your hotel, it can add a layer of safety, since it allows you to pick up a pre-programmed key card upon arrival. If you go to check-in and the concierge says your room number out loud – and there are people around – ask for a different room. A smart concierge will point to a room number and not compromise a guest's privacy. You do not want people to know that you are alone, much less what room you are staying in.

57

Ask for a room that is not near an exit or elevator

This might seem counterintuitive, but thieves look for rooms closest to the exits so they can make a fast escape. Ideally, you want a lower level floor, but not on the first floor. A lower-level floor is closer to the ground in the event of a fire or natural disaster, but not nearly as vulnerable as the first floor, in terms of crime.

58

Ask a hotel employee if there are any areas you should avoid

A concierge can be your best travel friend and ultimate insider to a destination. We make a habit of cozying up to female employees of where we are staying to get the local scoop. They will tell us where to go, where to avoid, and when. If you want to go the extra mile, bring small tokens of appreciation that are unique to your state or hometown. (Flight attendants love this too.) Never underestimate the power of women looking out for other women.

59

Let other passengers hit their floor first

If you board an elevator with a bunch of guys, make sure they press their floors first. We have had men follow us out of the elevator and try to muscle their way into our hotel room. The less information strangers have about your whereabouts, the better.

60

Check all the locks

Every time you enter your room, be sure to check all door and window locks (and locks to any adjoining rooms). Always use the safety bar on the door, and for extra security, bring a rubber door wedge. They are cheap, take up minimal space, and are highly effective.

61

When pre-ordering breakfast, do not identify yourself as a woman alone

When filling out room service selections on the hangtag you leave on your doorknob, only fill in your initials or your last name. There is no need to advertise your gender or that you are traveling alone.

62

Leave valuables in your hotel room

Expensive gear, such as your laptop, is more secure in your room or hotel safe than on your person in a day pack on the streets. Theft happens, of course. But you are far more likely to tempt sticky-fingered folks when your valuables are in plain sight.

63

Leave a note in your hotel

If you are going out, leave a quick note with your plan in an easy-to-spot place, like a desk or bedside table. If something were to happen, details of where you were going and who you were meeting could come in handy.

When you land in a new city, sign up for a walking tour of the neighborhood where you are staying. It's a great way to get comfortable in your new "home" and an opportunity to find local restaurant gems. Check out Airbnb Experiences for local tours.

- Amanda Lipnack, life coach

64

Walk this way

The best way to explore a new place is by foot. You get to see daily life unfold before your eyes, and may even stumble on a cute café, boutique, or gallery you would've missed if you'd gone strictly by a guidebook. The other bonus about walking is that the steps add up fast – and you barely even notice.

65

Be aware of your surroundings

Before you can determine if something (or someone) is out of place, you need to know what the norm is for your destination. The best way to establish a baseline of normality in a new place is to spend some time there and simply observe. Once you have gotten a handle on the normal pace of things, you are more likely to identify what is not right. Trust your instincts. Too often, we underestimate our ability to sense danger and ignore all sorts of alarm bells in our heads. Always have a plan in place for getting out of a potentially dangerous situation when your instincts kick in.

66

Be careful around ATMs

If you are in a foreign country, you may need to use an ATM to get out some cash. No big deal, right? You know the basic gist of how ATMs work, even if the instructions are in a different language. Be aware of friendly locals who may offer to help you use the machine. They may be phishing for your PIN number. Always keep your card number hidden and use your hand to cover the keypad when entering your PIN number. If you are worried about the security of an ATM machine, make your transaction inside the bank.

67

Split up your cash

Divide up your money in case you are robbed so that you do not lose everything. If you go out for the day, make sure to bring only the cash you will need plus a credit card. Stash your remaining money, a back-up credit card, and your passport in a secure place where you are staying. (Empty cardboard tampon applicators work especially well.) This way, if you lose your bag or get pickpocketed, your other money and travel documents will be safe.

68

Be mindful of local customs and dress norms

As much as we encourage creative fashion, sometimes that super-cute outfit you want to snap for Instagram can be a cultural faux pas. Pay attention to how locals do things. Whether it is personal conduct or what they wear, try to dress appropriately and go with the (local) flow. This means wearing a headscarf in some places and minding your hemlines in others. This can also be important when going to religious or historical sites – many mosques, temples, and cathedrals have a dress code they expect visitors to follow. In a perfect world, we could wear whatever we want, but cultural sensitivity is critical, and sometimes, blending in is a safer option than sticking out.

I have not found wearing a fake wedding ring to be completely effective, but it doesn't hurt. Just be aware of whether it's customary to wear the ring on your right or left hand in the country you're visiting.

- Antonia Hall,

psychologist, and global traveler

69

Consider wearing a fake wedding ring

No one should have to fake marital status when they are traveling solo, but unfortunately, it is a reliable way to avoid unwanted attention. You do not have to wear it all the time but having a spare ring on hand that looks like a wedding ring can give you peace and quiet in a pinch. It can also convey to strangers that someone is coming to meet you at some point in your travels – or at least, checking in with you regularly.

70

Wear your engagement ring wisely

This may seem a bit overkill, but you can never be too cautious when it comes to meaningful items. When traveling through local markets and train stations, turn your engagement ring around, so the stone of the ring faces the palm of your hand. In some parts of the world, a typical hustle is to be surrounded by mothers and children who will reach for your hand, and in the blink of an eye, whisk off your ring. If you feel safer leaving your ring at home, by all means, do so.

71

Attend local events

One of the best ways to soak up the energy of a new city or town is to attend a local event, like a concert, pub crawl, farmers market, or sporting event. Don't miss out on cool social outings, just because you're flying solo. There are always strangers you can engage with, and who knows? You may even make a new friend.

72

Check-in regularly

We are all for accountability. In addition to leaving documents with someone at home, schedule regular check-ins either via phone or email. You should not feel pressure to be in touch constantly, but it's a wise idea to give a heads-up to someone when you head out for the day, whether it's hotel staff or a quick text to someone at home. That way, if someone does not hear from you by such and such a time, they know when actually to worry.

73

Be careful around Wi-Fi hubs

Accessible — even free — Wi-Fi is great, but an open network can put travelers at risk for online identity theft. Wi-Fi hubs are prime spots for hackers to access your computer. If you are in a public space and you see an unsecured Wi-Fi connection (airports, train stations, cafes, and hotels all fall into this category), proceed with caution. If possible, opt for secure, password-protected Wi-Fi connections whenever possible.

74

You can also install a Virtual Private Network (VPN)

A VPN enables users to connect to a remote server and direct traffic through a secure network. It encrypts all your online date, so other users cannot steal your usernames, passwords, credit card numbers, browser cookies, and other identifying information.

We recommend SaferVPN (starts at $2.50/ month; iOS, Windows & Android).

Being in the moment now and posting about the moment later allows you to be fully immersed while keeping you safe from potential stalkers. Other than your mom – or another emergency contact – no one should know your exact location at any particular moment.

- Jenny Brown

75

Think twice before posting to social media

You want to share the play-by-play of your adventures (and maybe brag a little bit) – we totally get it. But you do not want would-be predators to know your whereabouts in real-time, especially if you are using hashtags like #solofemaletraveler. Instead, wait until you leave a bar, event, landmark, or restaurant to post to any social media platforms. Instant (virtual) gratification isn't worth compromising your personal safety.

76

Smile and say hello

Writer William Arthur Ward once said, "A warm smile is the universal language of kindness." It is the simplest way to meet people. But, in some countries, like China, people are not used to strangers smiling, waving, or saying "hello." So be nice, but don't take it personally if your actions are unreciprocated.

I love to see a young girl go out and grab the world by the lapels. Life's a bitch. You've got to go out and kick ass.

- Maya Angelou

77

Fake it 'til you make it

To have a great solo trip, you need to be in the right mindset. If you go out into the world and project confidence (even if you don't legit feel it inside), you are less likely to attract people who may take advantage of you. The few times we have run into travel snafus, we admit, we've looked lost, vulnerable, or simply weren't paying attention to our surroundings.

78

But, if something does not feel right, leave

If you feel uncomfortable with something, listen to your gut. It is one thing to push your first-world comfort zone, but you should never stick out a weird or potentially unsafe situation just because you do not want to offend someone.

To awaken quite alone in a strange town is one of the pleasantest sensations in the world.

- Freya Stark

79

Just because you are alone, does not mean you are lonely

As the saying goes: Wherever we go, there we are. This is especially true when you travel solo. It does not mean isolating yourself from the rest of the world, though it is likely you will experience stretches of solitude. That's OK. There will still be plenty of opportunities to connect with others.

Don't be afraid to meet locals. This means resisting the urge to bury your head in your phone, as it closes you off to any conversations you might have with locals, who might be willing to tell you about the best spots in town or a local meal you must try. I like having a few ready questions in the local language, to open up dialogue and see where it takes me.

- Kristen Gill,
travel writer, https://kristengill.com or
Instagram @TheGiller

80

Talk to locals

Talking with locals can give you greater insight into what they think, do, and what day-to-day life is like in a destination. You can meet folks organically or put out an all-points bulletin (APB) on social media networks before your arrival to see if people want to hang out or offer some local advice.

Take yourself to the city's public library. More than books, it's a free resource to discover a city and has many benefits like art and history exhibitions, gift shop, café, free Wi-Fi and, especially welcome on vacation, a quiet place.
- Waheeda Harris, freelance journalist

81

Live like a local
(while traveling like a tourist)

This may sound kinda cliché but doing the everyday things that locals do can create a deeper connection to a place. Shop the local supermarkets and buy new-to-you ingredients to cook with, take a run in the nearest park, sit for hours at cafés people-watching, or stroll into random bookstores and skim all the local magazines. Letting yourself get lost where locals live and spend time is the surest way to feel like a local.

82

Use the bathroom when you can

And not just when you need to. If you are traveling abroad, learn how to ask where the nearest bathroom is in the local language. Charmin, the toilet paper manufacturer, actually has an app, Sit or Squat: Restrooms Near Me! that lists more than 100,000 bathrooms that are rated for cleanliness ("sits" in green; "squats" in red). It's always a good idea to have tissues and hand sanitizer on hand, just in case.

83

Have a solo hobby

A lot of folks are totally fine just wandering around by themselves in a foreign place. Others need some kind of activity that anchors them to their surroundings. For some, it is photography, learning about design and architecture, or taking a cooking class. If you are the type of person that needs a sense of purpose, define what your "thing" is, and find ways to go do it. It is one way to follow a passion and put a brand-new perspective on it.

84

If you are a student, take your ID with you

If you are between 12-26, the travel industry considers you a student traveler. Travel companies from Rail Europe to Greyhound offer student discounts. Your student ID can score you lots of travel discounts at sightseeing sites around the world, and even free passes – sometimes even when no student travel discounts are advertised.

When a three-week-long visit to NYC unexpectedly became a solo trip, I took it as an opportunity to attend as many free (or pay what you can) museum days and events as possible. I saw some amazing exhibits at the Brooklyn Museum, attended a massive art fair and even took some sex workshops at Babeland. Tip: while free museum days are listed online, if you're interested in a particular museum or organization, sign up for their newsletter to stay abreast of special free or low-cost events in the city you're visiting.

- Simone Paget,
a columnist for the *Toronto Sun*

85

Take advantage of cities with free museums

For museumgoers, the price of admission to some of the world's most famous institutions like Paris' Louvre and Chicago's Field Museum can add up. Instead, opt for cities where you can visit museums for free. In Washington, D.C., the Smithsonian museums and the National Zoo are all free, as well many of London's principal museums, including Tate Modern, the British Museum, and the National Gallery. Also, most major cities have dedicated free museum days.

Food is a shared language around the world, so even if you're eating with a stranger, you'll always have something talk about.
- Naomi Tomky, food and travel writer

86

You don't have to eat alone

While you may be comfortable doing a lot of things on your own, like visiting museums and art galleries (which can actually be more pleasant when done at your own pace), when it comes to mealtimes, dinner is often the most significant difficulty for solo explorers. You don't have to eat alone, though – there are lots of options to connect with other people to eat with. From restaurants with communal tables to cooking classes that culminate in a shared dining experience, you can always find company when you need it.

87

Sing your heart out

Karaoke bars are a great place for solo travelers. There are ample opportunities to strike up a conversation with strangers: "What song will you be singing?" or "You killed that Lizzo song!" Plus, something is empowering about striding onto a stage in an unknown place and singing your heart out. The beauty of karaoke is you do not have to nail every note, or even be good, to have a whole lot of fun.

When I vacationed in Italy, I updated my Tinder profile to mention I was exploring the country and was open to suggestions on what to see and safe areas to stay. I matched with far more men than I usually would knowing I'd never meet them, but curious as to their suggestions. I found a flat for 25 euros/day and discovered lesser-known landmarks, restaurants, and local events I would never have seen. When I got lost, Ciccio responded: "take the bus to the second stop, which will cost 6 euros." It was like having multiple personal travel agents. I felt safer knowing I had a throng of men I could ask questions.

- Wendy Harvey,
social marketing expert

88

Dating apps aren't just for getting laid

Sure, dating apps like Bumble, Tinder, and OkCupid can help you find a hookup. But they are also useful tools for meeting like-minded locals and travelers along the way. Change your dating location ahead of your trip and be clear in your profile about what you're looking for. (Tinder Plus is excellent for perusing profiles around the globe.) You may happen to swipe on a cultural ambassador who genuinely wants to show off the best aspects of their city. Also, do not overlook Instagram as a way to meet people with whom you have a lot in common.

89

But if you want to get laid, be safe

Obviously, you do not want your first blind date to turn into an episode of *Dateline*. So, use your Spidey sense if you plan to meet up with any sexy chat friends. Once you have made a date, let a friend know and share your phone's location (Life360 is our go-to app). And remember, it is much safer to meet in a public place than, let's say, your date's fourth story walk-up apartment.

In my experience, meeting up with other solo female travelers not only creates a buffer against unwanted attention and harassment you may encounter, but it allows you to share (and pool) the wisdom, wit, and savvy often possessed by fellow adventurous souls. Plus, there's always someone to watch your bags while you use the airport/station baño...and you may have just stumbled upon a new best friend!

- Corinne Whiting,
travel writer (Instagram: @travelcorx)

90

Meet up with other solo female travelers

Just because you hit the road on your own, it does not mean that you actually have to do everything on your own. If staying in shared accommodations, like a hostel or Airbnb, it's easier to make friends with other solo female travelers. Also, there are apps, like Tourlina, geared toward connecting solo female travelers with similar interests.

91

If on a long trip, allow flexibility

You will probably cross paths with people during your travels who will tell you about a must-see stop. Or maybe you will connect with someone you want to spend more time and explore with. It is okay to book things in advance but allow enough flexibility where you can shift gears on a whim. There are so many experiences we would've missed out in we had inflexible, non-refundable plans. There are definitely circumstances when locking down plans in advance makes sense; this is not advisable for someone spending 10 days in Europe.

92

Bring a bunch of postcards from your city or country

Whenever someone helps you out or shows you a great time, write a quick thank you message on the back of a postcard and give it to them before you move on. It is a small and inexpensive way to spread a little kindness.

All travel has its advantages. If the passenger
visits better countries, he may learn to improve
his own. And if fortune carries him to worse,
he may learn to enjoy it.

- Samuel Johnson

93

Think before you speak

Unless you are in private and around people you know, avoid making negative comments about your travel experience. No local wants to hear comments like, "Wow, I could not imagine living like this." Nearly 40% of the world's population lives on less than $2.00 a day. Travel is a privilege. Try not to be rude or disrespectful when you are on someone else's turf.

94

Don't ask people about their occupation

In the US, asking someone about what they do for a living or telling them about your career may be a casual conversation starter, but it can be insulting in other countries. There are any number of questions to get to know someone that does not pertain to their job. Chuck Palahniuk may have said it best in Fight Club: "You are not your job, you're not how much money you have in the bank. You are not the car you drive. You're not the contents of your wallet... You are all singing, all dancing crap of the world." The better questions to ask are: "Where do you like to hang out in your free time?" or "What is a favorite local dish that I absolutely must factor into my travel plans?"

95

Eating on the go is not the norm everywhere

Let's face it. People from the US live a fast-paced life and rarely slow down enough to enjoy their meal. In other countries, though, this can be considered impolite. Eating on the go in places such as stores, the subway, or museums, can be a major no-no, so take note of what locals are doing (or not doing) around you.

96

Never accept food or drink from strangers

This should go without saying: Never take food or drink from a stranger. I have had my drink spiked at a bar and was fortunate enough to recognize that something felt off in time to have a friend take me home. Keep close tabs on your food and beverages at all times. If a bartender or server does not directly hand you a drink, think twice. There is no good reason to compromise yourself, especially in the name of free booze. Date rape is a real occurrence, both at home and on the road.

97

Do not drink too much

When we travel, we tend to gravitate towards the nearest watering hole. It's the best place to make friends on the fly and get the local lowdown. Imbibing too much can dull the senses and make you vulnerable to others. When you are traveling solo, it is extra important to be cognizant and in control, so be aware of your alcohol intake limits and stick to them. To be safe, go one for one, alternating one glass of water for one drink.

98

Do not assume other women don't pose a threat

As a woman, it can be easy to believe that all the predators of the world are men. This is not the case. Women can do anything — and that includes being dangerous. It is imperative to practice caution when meeting anyone new, no matter their gender. The only time I have been robbed while traveling, was by a woman I befriended at a hostel in Panama – because I let my guard down. Whenever you are alone, there is always the potential to be taken advantage of.

Be sure to factor downtime in your itinerary, so you don't burn out trying to see and do everything. It's better to see less and actually appreciate it, and you need free time to wander, relax, and reflect on where you are.

- Susan Moynihan, author of *100 Things to Do in Annapolis and the Eastern Shore Before You Die* and founder of *The Honeymoonist*

99

Do not overschedule your itinerary

Instead of trying to see and do it all, conduct some pre-trip research and prioritize the things you absolutely do not want to miss. Make time for these things and fit in less important outings if and when time allows. As much as we like having a schedule, there is so much to be said for spontaneity. Allow yourself to wander, meet people, and stay in places a little longer than planned. Vacations are supposed to be a time to relax, unplug, and recharge. Try not to exhaust yourself trying to tick off a long list of to-dos.

100

Build-in time to recharge

If you are an introvert, you already know the importance of this. This could be lying in bed, looking at the day's photos, or mentally preparing for the next day. Take whatever time you need to relax and recharge, so that you can face each day with enthusiasm.

101

Stay positive

Of course, it's important to think about personal safety – there's a lot of scary stuff going on in the world these days – but don't assume everyone is out to get you. Whether you're walking home from a bar in your town or backpacking abroad, bad things can happen anytime, anywhere. Be smart, but don't let fear stand in your way of exploring. Leave your preconceived notions at home and have fun!

ABOUT
THE
AUTHORS

The best education I have ever received was through travel.

- Lisa Ling

CHARYN PFEUFFER is a writer, sex educator, and frequent solo traveler. Over the past two decades, her travel writing has appeared in more than 100 outlets, including AARP, BravoTV, Brides, The Globe and Mail, Marie Claire, Playboy, Refinery29, SheKnows, Sunset, Thrillist, Virtuoso, and The Washington Post. Charyn lives in Seattle with her dog Mimi, a rescue that she brought back from a one-month volunteer stint in Guatemala.

Her books include:
101 Ways to Rock Online Dating
Breast Cancer Q & A: Insightful answers to the 100 most frequently asked questions
Funk Shui: The Hippest Guide to Everyday Harmony
Color Cadabra!: A Magical Guide to the Power of Color

Reach Charyn here:
charynpfeuffer.contently.com/
charynpfeuffer@gmail.com
Twitter: @Charyn Pfeuffer
Instagram @supergoodsex
Facebook and LinkedIn: Charyn Pfeuffer

DAYNA STEELE, the creator of the *101 Ways to Rock* book series, is a Texas Radio Hall of Famer and former longtime Houston radio and television personality, a serial entrepreneur, and a popular success writer and speaker. Dayna also created *Your Daily Success Tip*, business and life success tips enjoyed by thousands of people and companies every weekday. She lives in Houston, Palm Springs, and New York with her "Wonder Husband" and various rescue animals. Dayna ran for the US Congress in 2018 in Texas.

Her books include:
Rock to the Top – It Now Goes to Eleven
Surviving Alzheimer's with Friends, Facebook and a Really Big Glass of Wine
Bring a Folding Chair: A Run for the U.S. Congress or How to Take a Seat at the Table (coming soon)

Reach Dayna and sign up for Your Daily Success Tip here:
www.yourdailysuccesstip.com
dayna@daynasteele.com
Twitter: @daynasteele
Instagram: @daynasteele
Facebook and LinkedIn: Dayna Steele

JENNY BLOCK is a writer, speaker, and the lead recruiter for *101 Ways to Rock* authors. She is the author of three books, and her work appears in and on a variety of high-profile websites and publications including *Huffington Post, Yahoo Travel, The Daily Meal, Playboy, Swaay,* and *American Way.* Jenny is also often called on as an expert for *Cosmopolitan, SheKnows, Huffington Post,* and many others. She speaks on cruises, as well as at bookstores, conferences, resorts, and many other events. She lives on the water in Southeast, TX with her wife and their chi-terrier Walter.

Her books include:
Open: Love, Sex, and Life in an Open Marriage
O Wow: Discovering Your Ultimate Orgasm
The Ultimate Guide to Solo Sex

Reach Jenny here:
www.thejennyblock.com
jennyeblock@mac.com
Twitter: @Jenny_Block
Instagram: @thejennyblock
Facebook and LinkedIn: Jenny Block

PUBLISHER CONTACT INFORMATION
LARGE QUANTITY BOOK ORDERS
SEND US A POSTCARD!

Daily Success Publishing
1400 McKinney Street
Suite 2110
Houston TX 77010
info@101waystorock.com
www.101waystorock.com

NOTES:

NOTES:

NOTES:

NOTES:

Oh, the places you will go!

- Dr. Seuss

Daily Success
THE BOOK SERIES